The publisher gratefully acknowledges the generous contribution to this book provided by Charlotte Hyde and Jean Sherman and by the General Endowment Fund of the Associates of the University of California Press.

NEW CALIFORNIA POETRY

EDITED BY

Robert Hass
Calvin Bedient
Brenda Hillman

For, by Carol Snow
Enola Gay, by Mark Levine
Selected Poems, by Fanny Howe

SELECTED POEMS

Fanny Howe

UNIVERSITY
OF CALIFORNIA
PRESS   *Berkeley   Los Angeles   London*

University of California Press
Berkeley and Los Angeles, California

University of California Press, Ltd.
London, England

© 2000 by the Regents of the University of California

Photograph on pages ii–iii by Ben E. Watkins.

Library of Congress Cataloging-in-Publication Data

Howe, Fanny.
  [Poems. Selections]
  Selected poems / Fanny Howe.
    p.   cm. — (New California poetry ; 3)
  ISBN 0-520-22262-8 (alk. paper). — ISBN 0-520-22263-6 (pbk.:
alk. paper)
  I. Title.   II. Series.
PS3558.089A6   2000
811'.54—dc21   99-33247
                                                     CIP

Manufactured in the United States of America
9 8 7 6 5 4 3 2 1

Grateful acknowledgment is made to the original publishers of the books from which the poems in this collection have been drawn: *Alsace-Lorraine* (Telephone Books, 1978), *Poem from a Single Pallet* (Kelsey Street Books, 1980), *Introduction to the World* (The Figures, 1985), *Robeson Street* (Alice James Books, 1985), *The Vineyard* (Lost Roads Press, 1988), *The End* (Littoral Books, 1992), *The Quietist* (O Books, 1992), *O'Clock* (Reality Street Editions, 1995), and *Q* (Spectacular Diseases, 1999).

Contents

Introduction to the World

I'd speak if I wasn't afraid of inhaling
A memory I want to forget
Like I trusted the world which wasn't mine
The hollyhock in the tall vase is wide awake
And feelings are only overcome by fleeing
To their opposite. Moisture and dirt
Have entered the space between threshold and floor
A lot is my estimate when I step on it
Sorrow can be a home to stand on so
And see far to: another earth, a place I might know

Hide the name away in the Secret

Jesus of the little Brothers and Sisters

Those born on the last day will have no name

But Mother, Father and the above

Till now the lips of hardened hearts used politics

To speak of love until they lost it

You couldn't argue with their logic

The oppression of realism is consensus

To those who raise what they value

Out of reach until it's magic

Sea mist surprises my heavy eyes
I know at last I don't exist
This register is only a certainty
If evolution's over and the created world
Is done developing this place
And its laws. Always fixed and free
You never know what you were or are
Expressing
Like mathematics around a head
On rising from a siesta

Small birds puff their chests and feathers
With the pleasure that they know better
High morning clouds unload themselves
On the world. Blue peeps through
Sunny boys have spacious souls but killers
Build war zones in the sky where they go to die
Blue poems. Blue ozone. A V-sign
Sails into the elements: an old ship
Named Obsolete though Lovely is easier to see
Now visualize heaven as everything around it

Concentrate on the top of the mast, father
Arms up. You won't be needing them
On the swaying sea to heaven. One last goodbye
Makes each hand impotent
Like false mirth or some stupid mutant
I'm off to see people because you don't need me
Yet, where don't doesn't ever mean never
And I'm crossing my own stony ocean
Consciousness has nothing to do with me either
I'm just moving inside it, catch as catch can't

■

There is nothing I hear as well as my name
Called when I'm wild. The grace of God
Places a person in the truth
And is always expressed as a taste in the mouth
Walking with your arms wide open
And 263 days to follow, four morning stars
And Yuri Gagarin orbiting Earth
I know I may never be found or returned
When Peter, Henri or Mary call me
Fanny, as if they know who owns me

Come, tinkers, among droves of acorn trees
Be only one third needful, O
Name the things whereby we hope
Before the story scatters. A cardinal
Is red for fever where you passed
The suffering world's faith
Is a scandal. Tests of facts
Bring dread to aptitude
You who loved the people and the world
Tell us our failings and if we're home

I am the people never so alone
As when abiding
in history, broken
No God but a causality moral
As a socialist. Success
Hardly ever exists on these nights
Which intervene in secret with a *don't*
and a *so!* For then I can't lead
The little into the day but run
Like a heart blind to advice

The sea at last lies over this place
And registers expressly
During my siesta
I know evolution is done developing
Its laws of mathematics must be correct
In my created head I don't exist
As rising bed-heavy the mist
Is fixed though always full of surprises
And the world in my eyes
Is hardly a certainty

If you have to die

Puff and visualize

The ozone of heaven

As easy seen high as seen through

And peep on the world as if it's obsolete

An old ship in new elements

Everything will sail into pleasure then

Unload your spacious soul

Whose chest full of killers is zoned

For the sun now in its feather blue building

When mirth sways like a mast

On top of a goodbye

I don't need oceans to move myself over stones

One hand up and arms

Which show I'm impotent

To people or some false father

Who have nothing to do with what I'm here for

Inside I cross myself

And concentrate on the consciousness

The sea comes out of

I'll pay and bow out
For not hardship but the judiciary
Connected the test of time
To penalty
I in my life spent my days
Escaping the creator, seedy as a man
Who disappears from his tricks
Now I ache at the strange
Creations, mine, which like women
Look new in the Court of God

Q

We moved to be happy

Like a remote sensing tool each body
in the family
adapted to earth's urbanity and travelled

When the water went south for the winter

it carried us down like storm-driven gulls
to this crash that we call a city

■

One black wing was blowing down the road

(Rain-washed road)

In the old days horses wearing green shoes
would trot on that grass

Our caravan has sought a remedy for memory
by moving over the same path

Snow rises as it falls

on small seaside resorts and on capital

premier personal country castle and well-equipped hotels

on pullmans flats canoes and fishing boats

on a fairy house and a crack house

on holiday and airport inns on tents and crypts and cars

and caravans

Roads end where only trees greet them

like brides in terrified feminine dress

I was sick of my wits
like the kids in *Landscape In The Mist*

hammered down into a sequence
like climbing onto a train
and sitting down

I had to keep moving the books around

After a good beating on a cold day
disappointment
slowed my recovery

Cotton replaced my lace
and peals of laughter
only overcame me later

when the ground covered
the way to my door like lava
and I really hoped

the hoping was over

Creation was the end that preceded means

Rain steamed on evergreens and ferns
in a larger darkness
than anyone could witness

A boy emerged from a cocoon
crying I have no right to be here!

Temperate gales blew from the jets
at Heathrow
where a baby was yelling so wide
you could see the typhus in his throat

You could also see a tall waterfall
and call it spigot because your eyes

(grapes on the palms of a saint's hands)

incorporated and diminished images
into little packages

Heaven has been my nation-state
safe sanctuary from the law
or else the production of hate and bread is not increasing

At least I know my tradition is among the contradictions

And rests upon a time
as close to never-was as anything can be

but still a story of something that almost came to be
the never-quite-but-hinted-at
attention of a Thee

Lambs don't fight being itinerant
or being where there are no minutes or questions
like Why be obedient to a world that will end?

Wool walks in the agriculture
ignorant of its coloring
Patented in blue yes as food and clothing
for persons and their furniture

Wherever I am becomes an end
Long drives through striped fields

when one episode includes the same
smouldering gas coals and glass as the next one
checkered with grime

A buried bulb
develops under these conditions the way mothering
turns the wilds into a resolution

The neo-neolithic urban nomad school of poetry
is almost for lone mothers only

Lines of us queue up
for a hand-out or to steal a pair of shoes
for this child or that

We know where we love by its stillness

Our task is to read the bedouins
now that we're lost at last

and can really see through words including me
to the other side that multiplies
the interior matter

I light up the grids
to make my woods

into a conservatory
Color all in to match the environs

If I follow a sequence of dares
each one will be part of

the final product
That's why I'm happy

■

A little clover's on autumn lawns

White petals bristle the way weeds build them

If goals create content stealth creates form

The air force hits space
with the velocity of a satanic wrist

How to give birth to children under these conditions
Favor the ghost over the father, maternalist

The Nursery

The baby
       was made in a cell
in the silver & rose underworld.
Invisibly prisoned
       in vessels & cords, no gold
for a baby; instead
eyes, and a sudden soul, twelve weeks
old, which widened its will.

Tucked in the notch of my fossil: bones
       laddered a spine from a cave,
the knees & skull
were etched in this cell, no stone, no gold
where no sun brushed its air.

One in one, we slept together
        all sculpture
                of two figures welded.
But the infant's fingers
squeezed & kneaded
                me, as if to show
the Lord won't crush what moves
on its own . . . secretly.

On Robeson Street
                anonymous
was best, where babies
have small hearts
                to learn
with;
        like intimate
thoughts on sea
water, they're limited.

Soldered to my self
  it might be a soldier or a thief
for all I know.
The line between revolution & crime
  is all in the mind
    where ideas of righteousness
and rights confuse.
I walked the nursery floor.
By four-eyed buttons & the curdle of a cradle's
paint: a trellis of old gold
    roses, lipped & caked
where feet will be kicking in wool.

            Then the running,
the race after,
cleaning the streets up for a life.
His technicolor cord
hung from a gallery of bones,
            but breathing *I'm finished.*
Both of us.

And when the baby sighed,
through his circle of lips,
                    I kissed it,
            and so did he, my circle to his,
we kissed ourselves and each other,
            as if each cell was a Cupid,
and we were born to it.

The cornerstone's dust
upfloating

by trucks & tanks.
White flowers spackle

the sky crossing the sea.
A plane above the patio

wakes the silence
and my infant who raises

his arms to see
what he's made of.

O animation! O liberty!

Robeson Street

The moon is moving away
As civilization advances without thought
For the consequences

Scattered snow showers put fine purfling
Around the edges of the lot

If I handle routines, I'll dream longer
Since the concord I long for
Is like not being alive but finished

Moonlight at a fountain
For extra cash and you won't see your politics
Funnel the soda

But continued actions will improve your looks
You whose last customer was Disappointment

After I'm done with it, the counter's
got a lovely brown finish

Solitary, I set up a night fork
And face the materials

■

A blight was on the oaks
in Franklin Park where Olmsted planned

and drew an artificial paradise.
But in the zoo an animal
killed his keeper the same night I wanted to kill mine,

and this stage was really hell—the fracas of an El
to downtown Boston, back out again,
with white boys banging the lids of garbage cans,
calling race-hatred into our livingroom

through leaves which naturally dizzied and fell

Flamingo pink on the chimney stacks
On bushes too beaten with snow
It's Saturn's morning, accumulation
During the single hours, enormous

Mixed clouds are more propitious than fleece
and the poor who are occluded
and stationary will tell the true story

A Millennium starts where you stand and cry
Oh man this life was full of failure
to say thanks
That unconscious body you're holding is mine
Open my heart for the night, it's empty
Three hundred and twenty eight more days
are due this year and even with that many lives

I'd still have only one history

When snow falls on Franklin Park
and black grackles—

North, South, Central—sit between
each invisible spot of
happiness—the mothers walk by, brutally

into the old autumn gush of rust
red leaves

like you should be lucky to grow old
at all. I still see them, more of us.

Puddingstone, rutty and tough, in snow under their feet
turns into a soft thing thrown down

over the edge of dried myrtle and beech ·
leaves. Cars whir and curse

in front of what used to be our house
before our fortunes were reversed.

This America is a wonderful place,
one immigrant said. If it's a cage, then it's safe.

Away from the park and zoo

    bends become
  calamities of bricked-up
  capital: those who
doze, mid-afternoon, meditate

bright close to time's receding

    glance and out.
    There's drink on the shelf,
grain in the pantry so the Padre
says it's not poverty we're getting used to

but it's just, he said, we got used to being

Pushing children in plaid & silver prams
us mothers were dumpy,

                        hunched in the damp

and our redlipped infants
  sucked on their strange fingers
    eyes stunned by the gunny-strong
      grass on near hills

I wanted to sit near sweet water, not salt
in the fuzz of extreme weather,
      but we're not here to

Like women who love the Lord on hills

what for what for, we cawed outside
    as in bare trees, too plain to see

48

In the sylvan section of the old zoo
		some of us pace and traffic,
			pushing carriages
up the avenue

while others do
		baseball and barbecue, near where
		the primate cage is closed

Birds pulsate in a repulsive
replica of the tropics as if painted, can't breathe.

It's the end of afternoon when all things blacken

		I say, Fix me a rum and coke
and a good strong smoke, Mr. No One
			Me and the kids are looking to go home now

Joy Had I Known

There's a lot of the West
On this continent
A large snow is drifting
Towards those parts and smiles
For the art pieces mounted on earth
Rebound as beauty in each thing is cut asunder
Steal the thunder of unclear weapons
And West is West even if you're in it
A US Space Station turns towards our ice palace
Those nearest the palace laugh hardest

Nothing in life is so exciting

As to be shot at

And missed

The cold now in the single numbers

Is shattered

Frost on my window glass

As if arrows passed

Snow, or a kimono, blows

Sleeves across your arms, crossed

Where you stand

Like an emperor driven into enemy camps

Matching and watching the Eros of the Universe

Outside snow decays the country
Browns of fertile mud's lowliness
Or the storms of Labrador
Blow the doors of heaven closed
The sunshine index drops to zero
and electric light is solo
Cheer along with other scientific things
The wind brings
Scattered flurries
Freezing spray and I'm living
When I hear your voice say *Joy*
Had I known before.

Veteran

I don't believe in ashes; some of the others do.
I don't believe in better or best; some of the others do.
I don't believe in a thousand flowers or the first robin
of the year or statues made of dust. Some of the others do

I don't believe in seeking sheet music
by Boston Common on a snowy day, don't believe
in the lighting of malls seasonably
When I'm sleeping I don't believe in time
as we own it, though some of the others might

Sad lace on green. Veterans stamping the leafy snow
I don't believe in holidays
long-lasting and artificial. Some of the others do
I don't believe in starlings of crenelated wings
I don't believe in berries, red & orange, hanging on
threadlike twigs. Some of the others do

I don't believe in the light on the river
moving with it or the green bulbs hanging on the elms
Outdoors, indoors, I don't believe in a gridlock of ripples
or the deep walls people live inside

Some of the others believe in food & drink & perfume
I don't. And I don't believe in shut-in time
for those who committed a crime
of passion. Like a sweetheart
of the iceberg or wings lost at sea

the wind is what I believe in,
the One that moves around each form

Close Up

The orange flower on the other side of that pane—
Paper or fate?

Put your finger in the light, Eyes, and draw
A white field. A lamb made of lambs

Before the world is round
There's a line of traffic
Which shakes aside all sparrowings

Triggers follow feelings but precede acting on them
A feeling triggers a feeling, then the heft
Of the hand to work

A human face is pressed on glass; mirrors like armor
Break shapes into targets

The woman's face on the other side of this pane—
Paper or fate?
Written in light, in either case

Conclusively

The night was almost too long to bear
Then there was evidence of mercy—a passing car—
milky air—and I could see
dry walls & gravel on the way to a highway
Atlantic for its grays

Loss is the fulfillment of the Law
Space collected on a long line

I was eliminated as a locus of mothering—
a she—physical but imaginary as a restless daughter

Why this body and not another

The one who came to destroy the works of women—their
offspring—
knew how many people were resisting incarnation
He counted on them by accommodating them

Guilt relieving guilt
is the get of killers whose mouths shine
I can't say enough about this—red because sore
& polished because wet

One died to become the spirit-guide
Before that time
there were second persons in everything
Then saints, then no one
to guide anyone to heaven
Cosmic expansion has gone in its preferred direction

I can hear the hour, this never
happened to me before
One day I will shake the blue sky from my hair
and slip back to consciousness—
the thing that is always aware
with or without a living creature to share its pleasures

Tonight I request the precious gift of final perseverance
shored up in my sheets
not far from a predawn holocaust
of travelling children

Goodbye, Post Office Square

Where wrought iron spears
punctuate the common and rain
turns to snow a minute
I learned six poems
equal the dirt in the road
twenty more make a cobweb
thirty five muddy bodies equal a wall
one and a half jobs don't make a living
great novels are stainglass
their pain is their color

Never welcome on the hill
I looked like a fool with my daily thanks
but the wine was my joke, it was really water
Two stones equal two kisses up there
a leather jacket equals a terrier

In the next world I discovered
a hovel where a naked I writes with a nail
There you're as small as zero, the hole in the wall
the mouse goes in
with a whorl of cheese
for the littlest glass-cutter to eat
To paint one rose equals a life in that place
and on the thorny path outside
one cathedral is equal to the sky

Lines out to Silence

How long I've waited, I can't count
Long days in green—eternal advent—

like fine bones drying in the north wood snow
when the whites of the hunter

have come and gone—
I'm animal mineral vegetable friend—

calling to one. It keeps me young.
Through rainclouds on the hills I call

down to the ivy, watery walls
past the gate, slate roof and brick

painted to childhood's size
To one I cry: Come!

Take the walk with me home.

No more cinders, the cellar water is iced over

Red squares have dropped off the log
with days of the Epiphany

Uniforms are thrown down and Jack Frost
paints up a storm. At dawn—alone—

I see the moon get lost in the west
dragging her skirt of water

behind. Is it too soon—or too late—
to put bread on the table, then chocolate?

To know joy in the bed
the hidden breath of spirit or hope

like a ribbon of childhood's hair in soap?

Amber is a fossilized resin, yellow
Chains of cork trees from China

end the arboretum. Seedless lemons,
unpearled mollusk, the danger's over

Our words are as bitter as citron, worse—
blank and deflecting

Hello's esteeming manner
where two can't lock together

Trailing the bill of a mallard
around the yellow reservoir
my hope was as weak as my vision
There was brick on the margin, it was twilight
where the city of Boston stood for a prison
    The path turned forever
    It was that uncertain.

Blue river, icy sunk
where something but nobody fell

Now theology is necessary
for the way there are these holes & questions

Père Noël, whose presents like questions
come from the mind:
Let me be helpless & hopeless this coming year

let me know God and not feel fear

Winter tones are rose & glass
the sun as false as all nostalgias
If this world isn't good enough for us
then an afterlife won't be enough

Dry is the word for a life of solitude
But a flood would be like a two-faced friend

one thing in a virgin forest, another in a garden
bed

As the moon is an alien rock
one who has attended history intact

is only an ornament

Snow be in this time with us as music
River frozen and twigs done
Lists of birds are etched into the birches:
white notes on a yellow scroll

A cross of light on the ceiling or wall
tells the room's a cell
Contemplation of white lines crossing

coos behind the wainscotting, if this is the end

it brings no surprise.

But if
never happened

Now: then
a new situation

No chance
for if

to come again

So then?

Unknown, unowned

Like the ghost of a woman from ruin
to doors with one pair of shoes

in a drenching rain
or when a spirit in bird-form hits the glass

I waved farewell by the lash
of my eyes, to say goodbye

to romance—once—and much time passed

No my furor
will never recover from that hour
ten years ago six months from now

I may never see the Vatican or Troy
but only let me sit in a car somewhere
I recognize as home by the hand
of the one I love in mine—

just once—O universe—one more time

Poem from a Single Pallet

The wildness of the flower is all in the tone
Where the yellow goldenrod's a chirrup

When its chaperone is sleeping, Queen Anne's Lace
appears beside chicory, seemingly for beauty's sake

And one wild rose, the last,
before October, blackens on the bush, the bees

have headed off to the thistle factory
It's audible, if you see it—

color & strain of voice, among purples,
an indifferent shoulder (rocks) raised to dim

the passionate voice

Three bags of gold, a fairytale—
says "there's three of everything
in this world," but don't ask why.
Three bags ablaze, but manageable

One is browner, rich and red
This is the bag of dream-analysis

One is pale yellow, or off-white, and this
represents the wish

The third is a glittering heap
of nuggets like some autumn tree

glimpsed in a sun's late mist
vulgar & true, this is the big

bag, the bag of forgetfulness
which lasts

till the weight of it breaks

But I, too, want to be a poet
to erase from my days
confusion & poverty
fiction & a sharp tongue

To sing again
with the tones of adolescence
demanding vengeance
against my enemies, with words
clear & austere

To end this tumultuous quest
for reasonable solutions
to situations mysterious & sore

To have the height to view
myself as I view others
with lenience & love

To be free of the need
to make a waste of money
when my passion,
first and last,
is for the ecstatic lash
of the poetic line

and no visible recompense

The Vineyard

To imitation England

Her owners brought her
Something like a transplanted hand
Of green fans grew in the vineyard
And she was there. Despair
Calculated she'd be home by never
When she was looking to locate
Heaven under a bell of seeds
She found her bird, they'd hung it there

By a bottle of fatigued blue flowers

And a black butterfly

One owner wondered which copy of two selves
Was better
Suited to a good harvest
A free self belonging to the whole world
Or a married one under the law
It was a bird who answered
Sitting recluse: woodsy: the hidden one

In a workplace torn by a union

One angry worker
Picks with curses

The other
With wine in hand
Pays the picker of the vines
The same as children
Both servant and served
To the parents born with them

Red X, correction. Red check, yes.

Xero, xero, xero
Like so many bloodied lambs
Up in the air suffering
And sex continue
Some selves find freedom in counting
Others run away from numbers
Without a mind there's none of either
But copy, copy, copy

■

All night the rain

Pelts the big leaves
Kids are in peril skidding
In puddles cars turn over
The woods snap into parts of light
The city stays hard and high
Cone shapes predominate
In each landscape weights and shapes
Repeat the Father's name: *Not-this-Not-that*

When men wore overcoats down the stairs

They told their servants not to complain
Echo X was when your name was given
Echo A was when your self cried help
All the others were like the ears
Of a female or native
Too sensitive to every sound
In the secluded vineyard
The real voice is inviolate

The self is a servant only

To its source
Even when the mustache of a Justice
Shades the Bill of Rights
And everybody means well
Like an elf and a giant
At the communion rail who show
Equality is not material
But X amount of soul

To me the disobedient

Servant sobs like a child
Self first
Her throat convulses
And sends down salt
Between the dreams of one night and the next
There is only her bent
Dark head, raised knee, white shirt and the chair
He sat in last night turned towards her

Now a daring blue heron

Hops into place

And a cloud

Sends showers down

Some movements

Correspond

As if each thing is sewn into time and

Having a child

Is the most extreme caprice

When home was a courthouse

With Platonic halls and people
White as candle grease
Sight's escape went to green
Leaves and the light on
The window fronting the field
Lengthened her posture
As a child rose to the one on his way
To the door, the Justice

Liberty for the few

Equality for the many
The criminal copies the oligarchy
Which is an international fold of moneys
The gulls of New England
Close their bills against the oil
Spills. At night pleasure rocks
In chairs and harbors
Wine colors contort on the goblets

■

Fog grays the skyline

An orgy of terror follows
The tired humans
Turn grapes into wine
Their two-way grins
Wash up like a chance
To have faith in a giant when faith in the self
Has been lost. Twin appetites
Let no light in but refract it

One dreams of a land with vines

In purple or shadows on hills
Aren't pockets of mercy
In a world mostly stone
A constant elf—himself, herself—
Elevates song
To the day when birds will be angels
Again all senses precious
And light in the service of loneliness

The owners over the ocean sailed

From Mark to Karl and the angry
Gulls backed up into the sky
From nests among ankles
Of running selves. Some had never been
So free who had no ideology
But the ones with the goals
Ran after them crying
Kill them while they're still alive

Some selves are generous

Their faces face us
With ohs of vowels
Some selves sit at a distance
As if time had torn their feelings
From things forever. Some selves
Wake at four and some at seven
When certain selves act on their beliefs
They are given medication

Since tears become stones

Be fair to the small and raise each self
As high as it will go
Or things will be bigger than they
One day the help might become
The boss and earth let loose
Its silent members
Pebbles will roll over and insects
Pull on their gowns and shoes

■

Love's body and mouth lie down together
Its hidden parts soft inside
A right triangle
Its mouth is well made
Muscular and wide, I like
Its hands, long shadows in the joints
Both palms lined to show it's had some lives
All its hair prickles and shines
And its smile
Goes down. So does the sun

In the Spirit There
Are No Accidents

God is already ahead and waiting: the future is full.

One steps timidly over the world;

the other is companionable.

The house is there. The door is there . . . others . . .

But for you they make no sound when you're so far.

I know the bench is by the pond tomorrow

when I can follow the streets to it by heart.

Yes, streets. Yes, heart.

Nightwalk of faith, chromosomes live in the past.

The land is an incarnation

like a hand on a hand on an arm asking *do you know me?*

I feel the city grow wild with desire fertile

as turned-over sod in the zoo at day's end.

At the old Boston Lunatic Asylum

the windows are smashed, packs of dogs live in the
    basement,

elegant freezers unfold. Your heart you can hold in your
    hand

and did, approaching from the side, my head bent with
    shame

at having been in the world so long, and still feeling young.

We should have walked on the esplanade twenty years ago.

Now I know how to comfort a human like you;

then I'd have held one.

The first disappointment
was the first gift
as the second was the third.
Ongoing delirium of

open-to-happiness
ending with some white tree
and more such stuff

Eye those sights as ice hours
of distance, no access
through touch or guess.

No warm breath
or yellow rosing, nor sift
of sun, to say from someone
never to come:

so the biggest bang came
with an orgy of contact
suddenly withdrawn!

That was the last one.
A gate of a gift.

The constant X
equals all variables:
even strangers soon to be wonders
just amount to X
Cistercians, all 'sister' in any case
sexless, insist
the last & best
is left for X

So Wilde's little swallow
made children cry, don't fly!

But action is prayer
for the poor and/or
ill; just makes equal
stone and jewel

And X—
to everything else than X—
is just as much more

The indivisible heavens
have scattered petals
on the public lawn. They fly

into a circle,
soon spent & broken by
another larger pattern

A face breaks up this way
And 'invisible memory'
also has its parts.

Time is exhausted
faster than energy, it seems
to me, when some delicious wishes

can restore unity
White trees, say. Cherry, if
not snow

Sister Poverty, welcome to my cloister
All that lowers must draw close

In the world of wretches & the exploited
Of the accidentally destroyed

The strike of each heart
In the distant body
Ups the odds that there's a why but, why

Some patios won't allow the shadow of a maid
It's where I want to go with my tray
See heat unbearably white
Each book must fall, a scholar's mind
Like a shoal of mackerel
Will go through the roof. Now sleep
Is the container of all hope
Where underlover sends signals
To hang up the calendar
Face to the wall and to hell with the soup

It was a night to be left alone
To dig out fifteen pounds of pumpkin guts
Stick in a candle and water the curtains
I phoned a friend with What do you want
Money and luck they said
When I asked the angel in the bottle
She fluttered and cried
I want to die!
Sex, too, squeezes out a lot of pleasure
Till nothing is left but the neck

Son the One who was also called Sun
I crave your heat but fear the burning
Domesticate your fire and send sufficiency
Zero has gathered into a hole
By the road where living gives
An atavistic echo, the bank's
A thief. And I am without
Retinue. The feel of accidie
Is a collar, metal and economic,
When the world takes up no space but I

The Sea-Garden

Bricks are stuck in earth
By the potting shed where the gardener stands

Mother is also there, young enough to supervise and be
    superior
And sister is in thrall
At voices over the wall

She draws misfortune from the air; her mouth is as moist
As the spittle of a pea

Both worry about paying the gardener for years to come:
With sugar? With wine? She who got him to clear the
    vines
Says: "The voice makes a covenant
Among flowers and debts."

The human is a thing

Who walks around disintegrating. Robins
Take turns in the birch. Lower down, hottentot figs
Burst green water

I've got to try touching
A cactus

Never happier in the world—that—am
Happy as yellow monochrome
The fragilest color among them

Among brick pots, buckets and rakes
A row of inverted grape leaves climbs to a pale green

A flower is a little gardener

Sprigs and herbs
Make a function
Of wilderness in a world

Which can only save itself
By violent rupture from its own laws

Thin strips of clouds spill across watered yards, a nation
And spell Jeshua . . . Liberation . . .

The highway cuts through
A valley of mist and moneyed orchards

Oranges (suffering people)
Are packed in trucks under the sun

As much picked as packed
Till evening

In the drinking leaves
I dream of water as chaste as the Sisters
Who grew thin

So they could slip through the bars of a cage

Mother is often lop-
Sided, her face like a Cubist
Drawing or cubes of ice

Two shovels, two rakes, two hands

Even a prettier sister
In oversized overalls, saw
Herself twice as she was

Surviving on invisibility and powerful shyness
Work was all doubles
Down to the matter of time

Who asked, *Can I have a slave or two?*

Rapture in exile—paradox:
This garden's not a home

Red sun on heart-shaped leaves
Is like the heat of the true vine
But not it

To them
Who can't die without a mother or a man

The Quietist

Mad God, mad thought
Take me for a walk
Stalk me. Made God,
Wake me with your words.
Believe in what I said

Just shadows
Shadows on sheets
Grass, seed . . .

Push my anguish down—
Coffee, smokes & creams—
Tongue-dainties
To scare compulsion away
Compulsion to die

My bedclothes were stuffed with ashes
The spreads were incarnadine

Our match had burned at both ends
Since temptation concludes where the middle is nothing

Can a desire be a mistake?
The theme can be wrong, but not the music

And I lay there dying
For my asylum

Was myself

Two waters—squared
by an alley—

Three acorns—
One wet chair

Several yellow
chestnuts—

A man's erect
nipples

It was enemy class
travel

with the devil
who's red for a reason

Pleasure bloodies his underskin
Thin skin

The holy one called:
"Just keep that word in your mouth
Let the sound behind it out."

Slippery-like. Rain loosens dirt
From nails on the crucifix
And where the rose likes the mud it lives in

Smoothing cloth and chalice
When I taste "God" I taste bread

What does serpent mean?
Bite your own tendon

One has to die

The dirty parrot
On a bar in my brain
Means squalid. Repetitive.
Who daily says "clavichord"
Daily says "divine"

Sex is made on a bed which is too loose
Or too hard
Arrows & burning thoughts included

Some are more released by cords
Around their hands than intercourse
But either one

Will die if there is no pain

Zero built a nest
In my navel. Incurable
Longing. Blood too—

From violent actions
It's a nest belonging to one
But zero uses it
And its pleasure is its own

When she was alone in her cell, she didn't exist
Only bliss. Clay angels
Popped off the walls outside, one fate
For each shape, the highways
Couldn't be reversed

A maximum amount of randomness
—raindrops, invisible aerial holes—
Against a minimum amount of order—
Her body—compact—organs
In rows depending on use

Laughter—or slaughter—outside the door
And inside she was dying
To join in. So she had to go out
—a physical body

With subjective needs
Wing with the post-Christians. Her brow a headline
Reporting news of weather & mood

From masters of the military & amorous arts

Hide in her little close

Off the runway, or step into their story

O'Clock

After this girl was grown
the tedium of the nursery began.

Either overdressed or a mess
she was a metaphor
for the suffering of the Irish.

Seven boys and seven girls, a harnessed pony
and a clay pipe, delinquency laws and bad thin boys.

Out like a scout, she tackled the fields
in her hem or heels.

When she was dragged and staked
she called the story of her life
Where My Body Went.

Go on out but come back in
you told me to live by, so I went
with my little dog trotting

at my side out of the garden
into woods colored rotten.

I did this several times, out and in,
it was of course a meditation.

The out surrounds me now
a whole invisible O to live in:

tender tantrums, sky gone suddenly gray—
still soften light but no one brings

papers here to sign. The top of the water
shudders under the brush of wind.

Past? Present? Future? No such things.

A full Irish breakfast
consists of sausage, black pudding, brown bread,
butter, jam and some kind of egg.
The tea bag is dropped
into a stainless steel pot
and you pour steamed water on it.

Now the light behind the clouds is rinsing them blue.
And gales on coasts and hills
will fly from such a sky.

The earth will suffer, drop,
then enter eternal doubt
and those soft clouds

will be its literature.
Space in time goes against nature.

This condition is called "the future."

Every glance works its way to infinity.
But blue eyes don't make blue sky.
Outside a grey washed world, snow all diffused into steam
and glaucoma. My vagabondage
is unlonelied by poems.

Floral like the slow-motion coming of spring.

And air gets into everything.
Even nothing.

Hive-sized creams are on the chestnut tree
alive for—and with—bees—boughs
of copper beech gives birds a ride

for their whistles—clouds
course overhead—the gorse
is buttery sweet—it's May

—the day the right hand gives to the left.

While the lamb pecks at the tit
of its mother—it seems
the rest of the field has gone to sleep.

Now milk drips down its brand new lips
and bubbles of grass wet the ewe's.

She stops chewing and turns her face
to gaze at the feast at her waist.

Like a sheep sweating inside
its thick coat, the earth settles
and steams and lives by friction.

Sun ignites the skyline—clean green
after rain. Even wood
is sick for the heat inside it to be met

and I associate.

I suffer from ire, it's electric.
I quaff a philter to choke it—
followed by a cordial—

the next morning, my ire is back.

When was my heart's ease lost
in circles of fire? When I started
seeking cures made of poison, asp.

Next time I'll travel by dream.
Quick forward into first person.
I'll try to avoid the world
where bombs obviate everything.

The twelfth century was when?

Minister to my friends, Saint Peregrine.
Doctor to my family, Saint Joseph of the Hands.

Can obscurity be so fertile for workers
that they can grow a monument
from the thing in their fingers?

Grant me, Ma, the proletarian way to
perfection.

Then fold back my unbelief
as you did my sheets.

The dirt feels sweet
to the cheek of the sick.

When you're up against the grit
there's no more fear but fever
persists among fairy insects

and the smell of God is animal.
Cool grass is your nurse, and sandalwood.

The slit should be blue
and the solid part red

if it's daybreak and I'm good
for lying on now.

The light comes in to see
the children who make my knees

a pillow. As for the dogs
they slunk away with the guys

—not starved but replaced.

I think of the labor theory of value

as meaning nothing for mothers.
But what isn't a lie.

Soft fist of feathers
high to invisible
pulsing through May's misted sky—
Let courage
fly in me this way.

Stop, now the yellow
whistle's timid:

the little bird peals
with chirp-chasing beak,

cocks head
and's dittoed

inexactly, from trees.

Clotted cream and heather, Bronte way to heavenshire
—no, vanity's ugly place.

The sky is the mind and the mind isn't mine
when it travels the world as ambition.

Get up, girl.
A sun is running the world.

Under sky that is water
humans are humming—old to indolent.

One turns fierce and puts down the phone.

Pear trees wetten, petals fall.
A soft rain elevates the land and hands
long at working: two shake on a cane
and four lie still. All gone wild.

Rain—red rhododendron tree—
whitethorn—drumlin—you and me—
a hum of bees—tea—
white milk—brown sugar—bread—honey—
waterdrops—late afternoon sun—near Drum.

Inside me, a pulse of desire.
Inside me, the way elsewhere.

Where twigs are breaking stones
and red berries live next to thorns
I never am. I mean
where are the real ones?

Now as usual covering a view
through cool glass to wooden sticks.
If whoever wants to know.

Probably a branch is weighted down
by snow. Then who can see more of the red
than me? All the rest.

Half of every experience is lack of experience.

Parent above, look down and see
how far from you I've travelled.

From the swell in your firmament
you'll see the way that the light
has diffused the location of home.

I've lost it, roads wilden
into an interstate between work and wine.

A red shirt for anarchy.
A white mask with no face on.

The immersers have returned—
firebrands and no mercy from them.

Still, others ask: if your muse was a boy
you loved at age fourteen and if you didn't mistake

one later love for him,
then why this fear of men.

Into the forest I went walking—to get lost.

I saw faces in the knots
of trees, it was insane, and hands
in branches, and everywhere names.

Throughout the elms
small birds shivered and sang
in rhyme.

I wanted to be air, or wind—to be at ease
in outer space but in the world
this was the case:

Human was God's secret name.

Rambling snowmounds and still sheep along
Cheviot Hills, dense fog, dots of dirt,
snow-banged buildings, scraped fields.
Land pays the price for becoming human.

You float inside your water
glass among inverted tree
lines, gold and thin as wands.

Your time is really fluid—
or painted in fluid—
your limbs tiny and breaking.

Green leaves are like pages, waterized.

I can drink the image up,
or wait for you to do it.
Whoever acts, divides.

I feel like the end
of a long day
near Druid stones
and ghosts and hedgerows

thick as storms
where mist takes form
in a water garden.
It seems I am back

in Glan and want
to stay close
to childish things
like milk and sugar

in my tea, a mother
who calls darling
—to clouds darkening
the daily hills.

Sometimes it seems
my sight's turned in
on a place dark green
and undefiled

and I am as old
as the young
will ever be.
No, I mean wild!

You travel a path on paper
and discover you're in a city
you only thought about before.

It's a Sunday marketplace. Parakeets and finches
are placed on the stones
and poppies in transparent wrapping.

How can you be where you never were?
And how did you find the way—with your mind
your only measure?

Welcome television to this rug-ruined room.
Three hours of wet traffic
and car windows rain-colored stains.

Physician Goldstein blows up people praying.
How done in Hebron and with what humility?

The girl whose global baby's swelling
in her nightshirt already has an airchild named Dream.

The one inside her gathers its knees, then falls down.
Tonight I've left no light on for men

but the baby ones.
To know anything new is to know it as known.

Iced stones in a nice hotel
Whiskey and jacket potatoes.

Through the porthole to the polar:
whisk-brooming snows
shred into the wind, *hello*
to the Scottish Highlands

where, in utter dismemberment,
the spirit unfolds to the animal
of its form.

When was when
we knew that what
we knew
      for the first time
we knew
      would be disproved
      by the end and then found
to be true again

The edge of the dome is slipping
like a fool's pudding
under silver. It's dawn, I'm up

aggressively begging: God
give me a penitent haircut
and a cell—not a hospital—

to defend my errors in.
And no answers, please, to any of my questions.

Sometimes a goodbye

seems a bee's
done buzzing

earily: purrs
in hair, furred

for the sting.
Fear's then

a hurt-leap.
Time comes in

like the words
Sit down.

Your nerves
reverses.

From the bray of gray donkeys
over residential walls

to horses walking
city paving with the sound

of cans popping open—
I can smell turf, bread and other goods—

tea and cigarettes too
in brilliant rain-sprayed gardens—

the ones where my mother
was a child among children—

and there I am finally safe
in the sensorium of Drum.

Prosaic poetry—an animal
with wings. Get her up the streets
to the narrowing.

There she'll know
what the common good means. As if things
grew closer to the glaze
of their associations.

Production continues into the alienated night.
The first movement of a message

bodiless as light.
I mean, produce, distribute, then recoup

your losses.

Are you worth your place in space
is all the day-boss wants to know.
Emotional time is what is irrecoverable.

Wild garlic flowers
whiten the forest—children love their brothers—

people are hope-filled—and skuthers
of wind wear down the quarries.

And worries wear down the man aging
to something as light as a trout

but more lonely from breathing.

The limits have wintered me
as if white trees were there to be written on.

It must be purgatory
there are so many letters and things.

Faith, hope and charity rise in the night
like the stations of an accountant.

And I remember my office, sufficiency.

The stains of blackberries near Marx's grave
do to color what eyes do to everything.
Help me survive my own presence, open to the elements.

Fog mist palloring greens, no demarcations,
but communitarian gravestones.

Celts lost to Anglo Saxons who endlessly defended marks.
Guerrilla war, terror:
the tactics for landless neo-realists.

Hello eternal life in the light
of Dublin sunrise.
Hope carries me as-iffing
up the hefty gaps.
Sudden dreams planted to what end?
Fertile as worms? Headless?

Bracken by the tracks.
Cold lard, layered clouds,
up-shaped sister oysters
return to their newly multiplied beds
in spark and lead.

I often believe that nothing can be lost.
A quarter-inch aura grows
like moss out of everything soft.

White crosses bleed into clouds where the trace
of pain is grey above Dunkirk.

When clouds over Europe float in layers
you can pray for a shining shower and soon
it will rain and poppies flat as paint

will lift their weights—evidence that
attachments survive through space.

When one more means one less, you are a drudge.
But bear down on passage anyway

and be a lonely communist.

"Why am I otherwise happy
they have blacklisted me?"

Because the divinity of yesterday
divides you from the evidence.

He was a cold-hearted Saxon
whose sex was as busy as a farm
and left the room warm
with the scent of hounds.

Believe me, he could have had it with anyone—
man or woman—but he wanted to be good.

These are the dangerous ones.

So leave the field
Overcast and gray as fluttering ashes.

Leave the lashing waves, Germans in church, take a walk.

Wouldn't you know it. The neutrality of the law
ends in punishment.
So pass through the wicket to where the lawn

becomes a thicket
crawling with roses in a halo of losses.

If you mess up, run to the west
and hide in its sunset.

Pretend invisibility
can be opted for

when it's everywhere
until you want it.

If you need to get lost, go underground.
There you grow strong and fertile as a slum.

Moon ink is too bright to read.

You run your fingers over the print
and get some sense.

But then you lose it too.
It swims in a pool of logic

that you can't disprove
because it doesn't move.

■

Inked-in
nerve endings
never by owner seen.
Snow-lit
like the house of suffering
known by no one but who's in.

I have backed up
into my silence

as inexhaustible as the sun
that calls a tip of candle
to its furnace.

Red sparks hit a rough surface.
I have been out—cold—too—long enough.

In envy's carriage there's a witness.

No it. Is true. In envy's travels
there are many new heavens.
But one little head goes everywhere whining.

There is a city of terror where
they kill civilians outside

restaurants—guys
who are fathers and things.

Food is a symbol of class there
and cars are symbols of shoes.

People are symptoms of dreams.
Bombs are symptoms of rage.

Symbols—symptoms—no difference

in the leap to belligerence.

Late afternoon—the shadows lengthen—
it's spring and mayflowers—blue and pink—are back.

Twilight looks like a park before a black part
comes down—for four hours only—when
you can hear the ones you came from say:

Dread the coming day.
Repress your ecstasy or you might die.

My hose ripped on the thorns
while the man was jingling silver.

A leg is all I remember of the horror, asking
Am I wearing nylon or am I plastic?

It was a pre-Christian transaction:
no value in facts.

Spring wind blows trumpet
vines & lilies across the lawn.

Cream drops float, then sink.
A cup tips. Happy lips
dimple at the rim.

A checkered cloth is spread
over wood like a coffin.

Complex indications for one she
stuck in a century.

Pass the small churchyard hamlet
with its dirty coats on. What's all this patience for?

I live at a level of barking.
Then comes the Burren with its silver showers
and underneath are stalagmites made of calcite.

What's the name of that water anyway?
Divers swim underground seeking meaning
in the absolute blackness.

Huge golden torches on the way to Finbar's ashes.

Converse airwaves
flail the sea where a trough meets high water

and the fall
of clouds conceals my view of the road.

My head is a windshield
fogged over with gas and news of the world.

Massacres continue in Greysteel and Palestine.
What is the Greek for complete as in done?
Even in this mess I can find a song to suffer from.

Then I can try regular sound, and then no sound.

Nuns, monks and swamis
have fought this same anxiety.
(No meaning. No interiority.)

The whole body
condenses to isolation and exhaust

as if neutrality in nature
prefers indifference

or thinks it does.

Unmanned ship—a bed
pressed with linen

for travelling women—
sheets to the wind—

who decided to fly
under dreamish conditions—

airy and solitary
—not here—not there—but always between.

Sallying off to the pub

over cowpads and dung
I was only describing
the person I'd become:

—a disturbed equilibrium
—individual of unre-Marxed belief system
—Carmelite
—mummy

But those were motives, not a defense.

Herds of deer wander—their heads like wands
upraised for fear
of the human coming—and we always do.

Whitethorn twists into torn lace
on the edge of brittle daisies who face
the sun without a blush.

Almost every prediction has come to fruition.

A war occurred in the vicinity
of a dream—the form of a bomb
in the hand of a man.

Not one idea but military crosses
clacking. Booted steps

blacked more terror than there was time
to give to the children names.
In the world of the dream

hope was like rain in a shell
or a skull
and each "I" was numbered
"1" in that Hibernia of math, no mothers.

On azure seats
chopped lights and limbs, big white sheets.

My day might be the museum of itself
Like I am an ancient mummy.

The avant garde worships history, the others
choose mystery. So far, God, this may be my last
book of unreconstructed poetry.

I won't be able to write from the grave
so let me tell you what I love:
oil, vinegar, salt, lettuce, brown bread, butter,
cheese and wine, a windy day, a fireplace,
the children nearby, poems and songs,
a friend sleeping in my bed—

and the short northern nights.

Most of the continent
will have unsettled weather today.

Thundery outbursts
from Minsk to Algeria.

Showers over Flemish fields
will sog the paths the closer they get
to the sea. The day should end.

Index of First Lines

Designer Nicole Hayward

Compositor BookMatters

Text 10/17 Janson

Display Akzidenz Grotesk

Printer + Binder Maple-Vail Book Manufacturing Group